P9-CBU-950

the weekend crafter®

# Painted Furniture

# Painted Furniture

## New Looks in Faux Finishing, Texturing, Stenciling & More

## LYNA FARKAS

**LARK BOOKS**

A Division of Sterling Publishing Co., Inc.
New York

**EDITOR:**
KATHERINE AIMONE

**ART DIRECTOR AND PRODUCTION:**
STACEY BUDGE
HANNES CHAREN

**PHOTOGRAPHY:**
STEVE MANN
SANDRA STAMBAUGH (PAGE 73)

**COVER DESIGN:**
BARBARA ZARETSKY

**ILLUSTRATIONS:**
ORRIN LUNDGREN

**ASSISTANT EDITOR:**
ANNE HOLLYFIELD

**PRODUCTION ASSISTANCE:**
SHANNON YOKELEY

**EDITORIAL ASSISTANCE:**
NATHALIE MORNU
DELORES GOSNELL

## DEDICATION

To my mom, with love.

10 9 8 7 6 5 4 3 2 1

First Edition

Published by Lark Books, a division of
Sterling Publishing Co., Inc.
387 Park Avenue South, New York, N.Y. 10016

© 2004, Lyna Farkas
Distributed in Canada by Sterling Publishing,
c/o Canadian Manda Group, One Atlantic Ave., Suite 105
Toronto, Ontario, Canada M6K 3E7

Distributed in the U.K. by Guild of Master Craftsman Publications Ltd., Castle Place,
166 High Street, Lewes, East Sussex, England
BN7 1XU
Tel: (+ 44) 1273 477374, Fax: (+ 44) 1273 478606, Email: pubs@thegmcgroup.com, Web:
www.gmcpublications.com

Distributed in Australia by Capricorn Link (Australia) Pty Ltd.,
P.O. Box 704, Windsor, NSW 2756 Australia

The written instructions, photographs, designs, patterns, and projects in this volume
are intended for the personal use of the reader and may be reproduced for that pur-
pose only. Any other use, especially commercial use, is forbidden under law without
written permission of the copyright holder.

Every effort has been made to ensure that all the information in this book is accurate.
However, due to differing conditions, tools, and individual skills, the publisher cannot
be responsible for any injuries, losses, and other damages that may result from the use
of the information in this book.

If you have questions or comments about this book, please contact:
Lark Books
67 Broadway
Asheville, NC 28801
(828) 253-0467
Printed in China

All rights reserved

I-57990-497-1

# CONTENTS

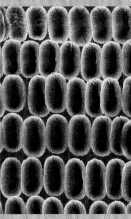

# INTRODUCTION

When I was ten, I had my first experience of transforming a piece of furniture from ordinary to exciting. My old wooden dresser looked drab to me, and, of course, I wanted it to be "pretty." Mom agreed to let me change it if I could find some paint in the garage. I may not have started a trend with my neon green dresser with bright orange drawers, but the feeling of creative achievement spurred me on. From that point on, I was hooked on painting furniture!

Now that I get to play with paints for a living, my interest in sharing the fun and satisfaction of decorative painting has grown along with my skills. The good news is that you don't have to be an artist or painter to undertake the techniques illustrated here. Each of the 20 projects shows you, step by step, how to achieve a variety of popular techniques, including faux finishes, texturing, gilding, and stenciling, using paints, stains, and various other materials.

Whether you're a seasoned furniture painter, or just someone wanting to try your hand at it, I think you'll be intrigued by the different effects and styles featured. Plus, we've selected a variety of types of furniture for the book— tables, chairs, shelves, a bed, a screen, a garden storage bench, and more—there's plenty to choose from. I hope that you'll discover that painting your own furniture is a rewarding way to create pieces that resonate with your personal style.

Although the projects are geared to working with new, unfinished pieces, you can also use old pieces from your attic, a garage sale, or thrift store. Simply follow the directions for sanding and priming that accompany each project, and your piece will be ready to go with a little bit of extra work.

So, slip on your overalls on a Saturday morning, and, I'll bet you that by Sunday night you'll be enjoying a new piece of furniture in your home that's sure to give you years of inspiration and satisfaction!

# GETTING STARTED

The following section provides you with an overview of how to prepare your furniture for painting and finishing, the core tools and materials you'll need, and descriptions of techniques you'll use. Each set of project instructions covers all the details you'll need to create each piece without guesswork.

## Preparing the Surface

The success of every piece of finished furniture begins with proper surface preparation. If you neglect this part of the process, the paint can lift, peel, or crack, and your top coats can be easily damaged. For this reason, each project is prefaced with a short section on preparation.

### SANDING

If you use new, unfinished furniture, you'll have less sanding and preparation to do. Even though most unfinished furniture comes smoothly sanded, it may have some rough areas. Use a medium-grade sandpaper for getting at rough patches and edges or raised areas in the grain. Use fine-grade sandpaper to smooth these areas as well as to sand the whole piece. Always sand in the direction of the grain, not across it. Remove the dust with a tack cloth or a barely damp rag. After this step, you'll either seal the wood before staining it, or paint it with a primer.

If you buy pine furniture, you'll need to take an extra preparation step. Pine has sap knots and dark spots that should be coated with a separate sealer containing shellac or a spray stain blocker before applying an overall coat of primer. If you don't do this, the spots will eventually rise to the surface and show through your finish. To clean the sealer out of your brushes, soak them in denatured alcohol before rinsing them with soap and water.

### PRIMING THE SURFACE

It's critical that you seal your piece of furniture with a primer after sanding it and prior to painting it. An all-purpose primer can be used with both latex and oil paints. Depending on the piece of furniture, you can use rollers of various sizes and brushes to apply the primer, just as you would paint.

Taking this step prevents any grain or dark areas from showing through. The primer will raise the grain of the wood underneath after it dries, so you'll need to lightly sand

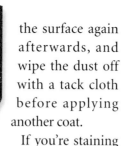

the surface again afterwards, and wipe the dust off with a tack cloth before applying another coat.

If you're staining instead of painting, it's a good idea to brush on a wood conditioner beforehand to keep the stain from looking splotchy. Wood stains soak into the wood and allow the grain to show through.

Today, you're no longer restricted to traditional shades: stains are now made in a range of colors. What's more, you can buy water-based stains that don't have the heavy fumes of oil-based ones. For some projects, we've used water-based stains, and on others, traditional oil-based stains. You can alter this if you wish.

If you're using oil-based stains or paints, make sure you're in a room with lots of ventilation, such as a garage that has a door you can open. You can also cart the piece outside if it's good weather. For extra protection, wear a protective mask and latex gloves.

## Paints

Paint is either water-based (acrylic or latex) or oil-based. Water-based paint is almost odorless, cleans up with soap and water, and dries quickly. Unless otherwise noted, we've recommended water-based paints throughout the book. Paints come in many finishes, but a satin finish usually works well as a base coat—the first coat of paint that serves as a background for other techniques. A satin-finish paint allows for easier application of finishes. Small rollers work best to apply the paint quickly and evenly on flat surfaces, while fine-bristle brushes work best on small areas such as chair legs. Always apply a second coat after the first coat has dried.

Artist's acrylics, purchased in tubes or jars, offer many color options and can be used to paint smaller areas on your furniture, such as decorative motifs or stenciled designs. These paints are more concentrated than household paint, and you may need to thin them slightly with water before using them.

Spray enamels can be used to paint furniture that is difficult to cover with a brush, such as a slatted chair. One color of spray paint can be used as a base coat, and, on top of this, you can create an airbrush effect with other sprayed-on colors. Always work in a well-ventilated space, and wear a mask when using these aerosol paints that rely on heavy chemicals to make them dry quickly and evenly.

## Using Old or Finished Furniture

Perhaps you have an old dresser from childhood that needs a facelift, or you've found the perfectly shaped bed table, but the color is all wrong. The first thing you need to do is take a good look at the piece of furniture that you plan to use. Very often, all it needs is cleaning and sanding. Sanding dulls the old finish and creates a smooth surface for painting. When you sand an existing finish, always wear a mask, and sand in the direction of the grain. If there are any nicks, cracks, or dents, apply wood putty to them with a palette knife, and smooth it out. After the putty dries, sand these areas again, and wipe them down with a tack cloth.

### STRIPPING OFF THE OLD FINISH

If the existing finish of an old piece is in sad shape—for instance, the varnish or paint is wrinkled or chipped—you might need to strip it first. Ask your home supply store clerk about the best product to use for your particular piece of furniture. Follow the instructions on the product. You MUST work in a well-ventilated room or outdoors, and wear gloves and goggles to protect yourself.

First, apply an even layer of the stripper to the surface with a bristle brush in the direction of the grain. As the old paint or finish softens, use a scraper to lift it off in the direction of the grain. Take care not to gouge the surface. You may find it easier to use steel wool to remove the finish on intricate areas such as molding and corner crevices.

## Basic Tools

If you've ever painted a room in your house, you already know a lot about the tools you'll need to paint furniture. In fact, you can get many of your basic tools at a home supply store. Check out those nooks and crannies of your garage or storage closet before you go out and buy more stuff—you might have some things on hand that you've forgotten about since your last painting project—brushes in several sizes, sponges, rollers, a paint tray, buckets or small plastic containers, a drop cloth, paint stirrers, sponges, lint-free cloths, sandpaper, a tack cloth, and masking tape. You'll probably use all of these things at some point. If you need fine brushes for detail work, you can buy them at a craft or art supply store. The tools that apply to particular projects are clearly listed under each project, so you can add these to your collection as you select the pieces you want to do.

which is formulated to dry more slowly than paint, providing a longer working time for faux finish techniques.

Before attempting a faux finish on a piece, try experimenting with color and technique—like the professionals do—on a sample board. To do this, base coat pieces of poster board or other heavy paper, and then apply the colored glaze to it to see the effects.

Our last project on page 73 introduces you to four finishes in one piece—a wonderful way to learn about glazes and how to manipulate them to create decorative effects.

# Special Finishes and Surface Decorations

In the following section, you'll get an overview of the many techniques that are covered by the projects. All of the "tricks of the trade" for each of these techniques are covered in the individual projects.

## FAUX FINISHES

Faux finishes traditionally imitate the look of another material, such as wood grains and marble. Many of the same faux finishes associated with interior design—such as sponging, rag rolling, combing, stippling, and feathering—are often applied to furniture. You'll also be introduced to some techniques that are now associated with this large category of finishes.

### Glazes

The faux finishes that you're probably most familiar with are done with glazes. A glaze, or wash, is a thin, semi-transparent layer of color. You can thin latex or acrylic paint with water to create a wash, and oil paint with turpentine to create a glaze. However, using a glaze medium along with the paint creates a semi-transparent effect. It might look milky when you open it, but it dries clear and won't affect the color of the paint. You can add paint or dry pigments to glaze medium,

### Vinegar Painting

Classic vinegar painting—a type of finish that's been around for more than 100 years—can give you beautiful surface effects. Initially, it was used to reproduce the look of exotic wood grain patterns on interior house trim and furnishings. The main ingredients are water, sugar, vinegar, and finely ground powdered pigment that can be purchased at an art supply store. Because this paint contains no resins, it's not self-sealing, so a coat of oil-based varnish has to be applied over it. This lack of resin can also be an advantage, because you can wipe it off with water if you don't like the results.

You can use brushes, crumpled rags, combs, feathers, and other tools of faux finishing to achieve interesting effects. One of our designers even used her fingertips to make an exotic pattern! (See the project on page 70.)

## Trompe l'oeil

Trompe l'oeil ("fool the eye"), a type of painting that dates back to the Renaissance, is now widely used in the field of interior design. Painting on furniture to create illusion can be accomplished with simple techniques or through more complex painting (see page 23).

Don't be intimidated by the idea of this sort of painting—you'll be able to easily undertake the projects in this book that teach you some basic ways to create three-dimensional effects on a flat surface.

## Texturing

Old plastered walls are now a soothing sight to those of us who long for a nostalgic touch, and many of today's furniture finishes reflect this mood. You can add texture to a piece of furniture with the same method that you would a wall—with trowel and plaster (or texturing paint). You can also sponge the texture onto the surface to create beautiful effects. With this added dimension, you can transform a plain surface into an intriguing one.

## Crackling

A crackle finish is a very popular decorative finish for furniture. To create an aged-paint effect, crackle medium is applied between two coats of water-based paint. The second coat reacts to the medium, and cracks develop on the surface. New mediums on the market are quite easy to use, and you can buy them at home improvement, art supply, and paint stores.

## Metallic Leaf and Metallic Powder Pigments

Thin sheets of beaten metal can be applied to the painted surfaces of furniture to create glamorous results. While leaf can be made from precious metals, it is also made from other less expensive metals that mimic the look of gold and silver. Leaf is applied to the surface by a glue medium known as "size." The size is applied to the surface, then allowed to dry slightly until it's "tacky" to the touch. The leaf is carefully applied and smoothed out on this sticky surface.

You can also buy metallic powdered pigments at craft or art supply stores. These powders lend a rich antique look to surfaces. Brush them onto a tacky coat of varnish before applying a top coat of varnish to seal them.

### STENCILING

Stencils can be made from sheets of clear acetate or heavy paper such as poster board or plain old manila folders. If you're using acetate, you'll trace the pattern onto it with a black marker before cutting it out on a cutting mat with a sharp craft knife. If you're using paper to make your stencil, you can trace the design onto it with carbon paper or graphite transfer paper.

### WALLPAPER

Segments of wallpaper on furniture can make a beautiful addition to paint or finishes. Any flat area on your piece can be used as a substrate for decorative paper.

Always cut a piece of wallpaper slightly larger than the area you plan to cover. Then, after you prime the piece, apply the paper with paste and smooth it out with a brush to remove air bubbles. Use a metal ruler and sharp craft knife to carefully cut the paper to size once it has adhered, and remove any excess paste with a clean cloth.

When you're finished painting and decorating your pieces, you may want to protect the surface and add sheen by applying coats of clear varnish or polyurethane. Both water-based formulas are available and come in a range of sheens from matte to high-gloss. Clear spray acrylics, which also come in a variety of sheens, are useful as a finish coat. When using them as a protective finish, you'll need to apply more than one coat.

## Sealing the Surface

When you've finished painting and decorating your pieces, you may want to protect the surface and add sheen by applying coats of clear varnish or polyurethane. Both water-based formulas are available and come in a range of sheens from matte to high-gloss. Clear spray acrylics, which also come in a variety of sheens, are useful as a finish coat. When using them as a protective finish, you'll need to apply more than one coat.

# Projects

*The following section features 20 projects accompanied by visual and written steps to make your foray into furniture painting enjoyable. Use the images and instructions as a launching point for your imagination and a coach for your technical development. And, don't forget that you can alter the colors of any piece to suit your tastes.*

# Watery Shelf

DESIGNER: LYNA FARKAS

*Use a simple chemical release process to create an aqueous effect on the surface*
*of this shelf. Watch the bubbles magically appear!*

Shelf table

Sandpaper and tack cloth

Water-based varnish

2- and 3-inch (5 and 7.6 cm) paintbrushes

Latex primer

Antique white satin latex paint

1-inch (2.5 cm) masking tape

Spoon

Spray bottle set on mist setting filled with water

Teal-colored latex paint

Denatured alcohol

Painter's low-tack masking tape

Small artist's paintbrush

## PREPARATION

Sand and wipe the whole piece with a tack cloth.
Varnish the legs, and let them dry. Prime the top and bottom
shelves, and allow them to dry. Sand and wipe them
down with a tack cloth before applying a second coat of primer.
Brush two coats of antique white on the top and
bottom shelves. Allow the paint to dry.

1 Tape a 1-inch (2.5 cm) border of low-tack masking tape around the edge of the bottom shelf. Overlap two strips of tape to make a 1½-inch (3.8 cm) border around the top edge of the shelf. Burnish the edges of the tape with a spoon to prevent the paint from seeping underneath it.

2 Spray water on the top shelf.

3 Quickly apply a thin layer of teal paint with the paintbrush. (The water helps the paint to float on the surface.)

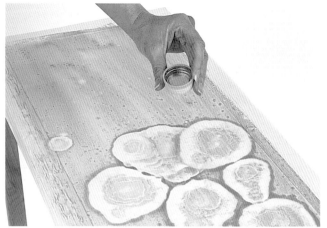

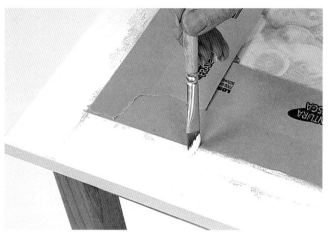

4 Pour denatured alcohol into the lid of the can. While the paint is still wet, splatter drops of the alcohol randomly on the paint. The chemical reaction of the denatured alcohol on the watery paint will create a bubbly effect. If you drip alcohol on a spot you've already covered, you'll create bubbles within bubbles. Continue until the shelf is covered with a design that you like, then let the paint dry. Repeat this process on the bottom shelf, and let the paint dry.

6 Use painter's tape to mask off the decorated area along the line where the border touches it on the top and bottom shelves. Touch up the borders with a small brush loaded with antique white paint, and allow it to dry.

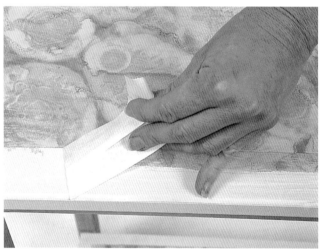

5 Pull the tape off the shelves.

7 Seal the entire piece (both legs and decorated areas) with two coats of water-based varnish.

# Elegant Chest with Gilded Silver Accents

DESIGNER: LYNA FARKAS

*Aluminum leaf lends a rich, silver quality that metallic paints don't. The simplicity of off-white with silver transforms this plain chest into a cache with cachet.*

## YOU WILL NEED

Small chest of drawers with removable knobs

Latex primer

Sandpaper and tack cloth

2- and 3-inch (5 and 7.6 cm) paintbrushes and small roller with tray

Off-white satin paint

Heavy paper

Craft knife

Low-tack masking tape

Soft-haired artist's brush

Water-based size (available in craft stores)

Cotton gloves

Book of aluminum leaf in sheets (available at craft stores)

Cutting board

Butter knife

Soft clean cloth

Shellac

Latex varnish

Silver knobs to replace existing knobs on chest (available at home supply stores)

Remove the drawers and wooden knobs from the chest. Sand lightly as needed. Apply a coat of primer, let it dry, and then sand and wipe down all surfaces before applying another coat. After the primer dries, apply two coats of off-white paint to the primed areas.

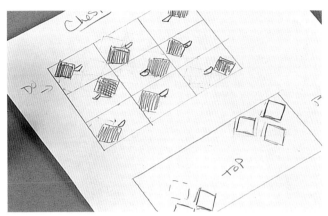

1 Do a rough sketch showing the placement of the pieces of silver leaf on the drawers of your chest, keeping in mind the size and shape of the silver knobs you purchased.

2 From a piece of heavy paper, cut out a reverse template with a craft knife the size of the leaf that you intend to apply. Place one of the drawers faceup on a table, and tape the template in place using your sketch as a reference. With a small, soft brush, apply gilding size within the boundaries of the square. Lift off the template and repeat this procedure on all of the areas of the drawers where you want to place a square of leaf. Use the template to repeat the design on top of the chest, following the same procedure. Let the size dry until tacky, or about 15 minutes.

3 Put on the cotton gloves, and take out a sheet of aluminum leaf. Position the leaf on top of the cutting board, and use the butter knife to gently slice the leaf into squares slightly larger than the template.

4 Fold a small piece of paper in half and gently pick up one of the squares.

5 Line it up with a sized square.

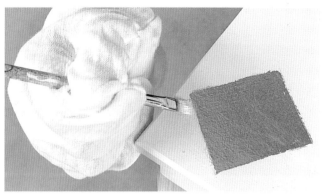

6 Gently press it down, working from one end to the other with the soft brush. Place aluminum leaf on all of the sized squares, and allow the gilding to sit overnight. The following day, rub the soft-haired brush over the gilded squares to take off the excess gilding. (Don't worry about the blurred edges at this point.) Wipe the area gently with a soft cloth.

9 Use a bit of the off-white base coat to touch up the edges of the squares where they are uneven.

7 If the size bled through the gilding along the edges, use the butter knife to clean the edges.

10 With a small, soft artist's brush, apply clear shellac to the aluminum squares to protect them. Allow the shellac to dry. After you've completed all of this, brush a coat of latex varnish over the chest and the front of the drawers. Replace the wooden knobs with the silver ones, and place the drawers inside the chest.

8 If a square has missed areas where the gilding didn't stick, apply size to those areas before patching them up with small pieces of leftover aluminum leaf. Allow it to dry.

# Verdigris Butcher Block

DESIGNER: LYNA FARKAS AND TERRY TAYLOR

*The painted legs on this piece appear as if they're made of brass or copper that has developed a lush patina. Add strips of abraded copper to the sides, and the look is complete.*

## YOU WILL NEED

Butcher block table

Latex primer

2- and 3-inch (5 and 7.6 cm) paintbrushes

Sandpaper and tack cloth

Flat black paint

Rust-red, copper, dark umber, and moss-green acrylic paints in tubes or bottles

Shallow plastic containers

Sea sponge

Small artist's brush

Latex varnish

Metal embossing foil or copper flashing

Scissors

Steel wool

Copper finishing nails

If possible, remove the legs from the table for easier
finishing on top of your worktable, or flip the butcher block
over and work on the floor. Prime the legs, and let them dry.
Sand and wipe down the primed legs with a tack cloth
before applying another coat of primer. Paint legs with
a coat of flat black paint, and let it dry.

1 Squeeze out a portion of rust-red, copper, dark
umber, and moss green paint in shallow containers.
Dab a damp sea sponge into the rust-red paint and
discharge the excess onto a paper towel. Sponge
randomly over one of the legs, covering about 75
percent. Apply the dark umber in the same fashion.

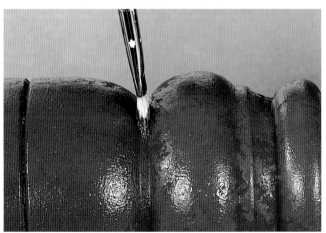

2 To reach crevices on the leg, stipple the paint
on with a small brush.

3 Use the same sponge to apply the copper, covering
the entire surface while blending lightly. Allow the
paint to dry.

4 Dip the sponge into the moss green paint, and
discharge the excess onto a paper towel. Apply
to about 25 percent of the surface, dabbing and
scrubbing it in certain places to give a verdigris
appearance. Allow it to dry.

5 To reach crevices of the leg moldings, use a small
brush to stipple on the green paint in a few areas.

7 Use scissors to cut strips of metal embossing foil or copper flashing to fit the sides of the butcher block, leaving a margin around each strip once it's positioned. Abrade the surface of each strip with steel wool to lend an aged look.

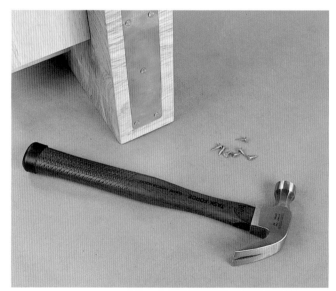

8 Use copper finishing nails to tack the strips into place on each of the four sides as accents that tie in with the metallic look of the legs. Reassemble the butcher block top and legs, if needed.

6 Repeat steps 1 through 5 to finish each of the remaining legs. After all the paint is dry, brush a coat of varnish on each leg, and let it dry.

# Trompe l'oeil Console Table

DESIGNER: DERICK TICKLE

*"Fool-the-eye" painting has been around for centuries, and this table will make any passerby look twice before discovering what's real and what isn't!*

Console table with drawer

Sandpaper and tack cloth

Water-based mahogany wood stain

Water-based maple wood stain

Clean, lint-free cloths

Ruler

Utility knife blade or small, flat screwdriver

2-inch (5 cm) paintbrush

Low-tack masking tape

Latex primer

Red satin latex paint

Black satin latex paint

Water-based acrylic glaze

Synthetic sponge

Plastic grocery bag

Water-based varnish

Clear acetate or heavy paper

Scissors

Decorative hole punch with design of your choice
(available at craft supply stores)

Rub-on gold pigment (self-adhering, available
at craft supply stores)

Clean lint-free cloth

Envelope

Artist's acrylic paint in white, yellow, brown,
red, gold, and black

Painter's wide masking tape

Small artist's paintbrush (liner brush)

Pencil

Black fine-tipped marker

Postage stamp (optional)

Key

Lightly sand the table to remove any rough edges or splinters, and wipe it down with a tack cloth. Apply mahogany wood stain to the table legs with a clean cloth. Wipe only in the direction of the natural grain. Repeat this on the drawer front and side panels using the maple wood stain. You might need to apply two coats of the stain with a light sanding in between.

1 Mark a 2-inch (5 cm) border around the edge of the tabletop. Use the back side of a utility knife blade or small, flat screwdriver to make a slight indentation along this line. Rub a coat of mahogany stain onto this border, and then dry brush a second coat on top to create a grained look (as shown in the finished photo). Allow the stain to dry. Mask off the border with low-tack tape. Apply one coat of latex primer followed by red satin latex paint inside the border to cover the top of the table. Let it dry.

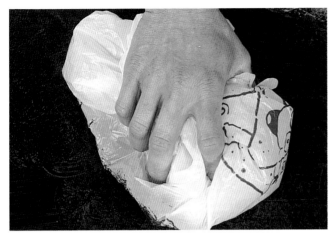

2 Mix a water-based glaze using one part black latex paint with six parts acrylic glaze. Wrap a synthetic sponge in a plastic grocery bag and squeeze the sides to create tight creases in the plastic. Apply an even coat of the black glaze to the top of the table. Stipple the glaze with the plastic-covered sponge, changing directions in order to create a natural leather texture. Allow the surface to dry thoroughly before applying a coat of water-based varnish.

3 From the acetate or heavy paper, cut a sheet that fits the curve of the table. You'll use this as a template for stenciling. (You don't have to cut a piece as large as the table because you can move the template around as you go.) Mark a 2¹/₂-inch (6.4 cm) border inside the curved edge of the template. Punch a line of motifs along the inside of the curved line. Position the template along the edge of the table, and rub the gold pigment onto the stencil with a clean rag.

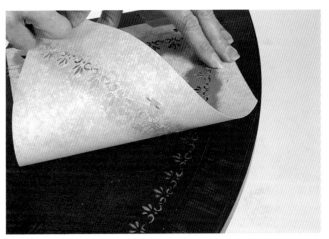

4 Lift the stencil to reveal the gilded areas.

5 Place the envelope in a position of your choice on the table, and draw a line around it. Tape off the edges and paint a coat of white acrylic paint inside. Allow it to dry. Use a clean cloth to smudge a small amount of gray (mix black and white paint) onto areas of the envelope to create the illusion of shadows. Remove the tape.

6 Use a small artist's paintbrush and black paint to create a shadow along two edges of the envelope, masking areas as needed.

7 Outline the shape of a pencil overlapping the letter.

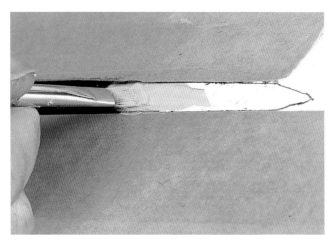

8 Mask off the sides of the pencil, and paint it with yellow paint.

9 Add shading with a bit of darker yellow made by mixing a small bit of brown with the yellow. Paint in the wooden portion of the pencil with brown lightened with a bit of white. Add a line of black shading along the edge of the pencil, and paint the leaden tip of the pencil.

10 Paint the eraser and band around the end of the pencil with a bit of red, and, after it dries, add details with a black fine-tipped marker. Finish the envelope by writing an address in pencil and painting or gluing an actual stamp onto it.

11 Place the key on the table, and outline it with the marker.

12 Paint inside the lines with gold paint, and add details with the black marker.

# Gilded Corner Cabinet

DESIGNER: LYNA FARKAS

*This quaint corner cabinet incorporates metallic powders and stencils on black to create a rich traditional look.*

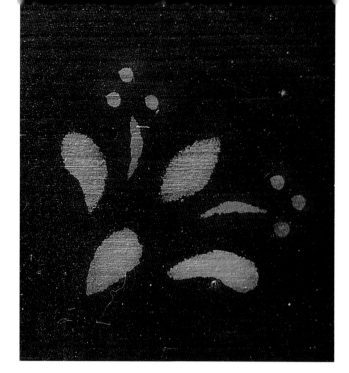

## YOU WILL NEED

Tall corner cabinet that has door with decorative molding

Latex primer

2- and 3-inch (5.1 and 7.6 cm) paintbrushes and small roller with paint tray

Sandpaper and tack cloth

Black semi-gloss paint

Low-tack masking tape

Oil-based varnish

Small paintbrush for applying varnish

Template (see page 77)

Manila folder, poster board, or sheet of clear acetate

Carbon paper (optional)

Pencil or fine-tipped black marker

Cutting board

Craft knife

Adhesive spray

Cosmetic sponge wedges

Paper towels

Small, soft artist's paintbrush for applying powder

Gold and bronze metallic powders (available at art or craft supply stores)

Cotton swabs

Mineral spirits

Take the door off its hinges so you can place it on a flat surface. Prime both sides as well as the cabinet's inside and outside. Allow the primer to dry. Sand it lightly and wipe it down with a tack cloth. Brush and roll on two coats of black paint over the primer, and let them dry.

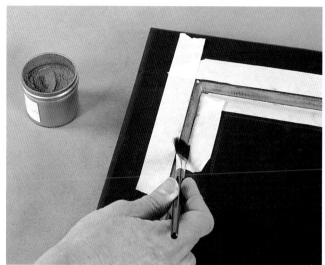

1 If your cabinet has a decorative molding around the edges of the door, you can accent this area with gold or bronze gilding. To do this, tape off the surrounding areas that won't be gilded. Brush a coat of oil-based varnish on the exposed area. Allow it to dry until it is tacky. Use the small brush to apply gilding to the tacky surface. Use this same process to gild the front edges of the shelves.

2 Transfer each template that you want to use to a piece of heavy paper or a sheet of acetate. If you're using heavy paper, trace the template on it with a pencil or pen and carbon paper. If you're using acetate,

place it over the template and trace it on the sheet with a pen. Position the paper or acetate on a cutting board, and cut out a reverse stencil of the design with a craft knife. (The easiest way to cut a stencil is to rotate the paper or acetate as you cut, and pull the knife toward you.) Spray the back of the stencil for the bottom corner of the door with adhesive spray, and press it into place. Secure it with masking tape as well. Dab a cosmetic sponge wedge into varnish, discharge the excess on a paper towel, and pounce upwards over the stencil cut. Let the varnish dry until it is tacky.

5 Add the gold accents to the stencil the same way you did the bronze.

3 Dip a soft artist's brush in bronze powder and tap the excess back into its container. Stipple the areas of the stencil that you wish to accent with bronze. Wipe off the brush when you're finished.

6 Repeat this process of varnishing and stippling to add designs to other areas of the cabinet. Lift each stencil from one corner to the other to remove it.

4 Dip the end of the brush in the gold powder.

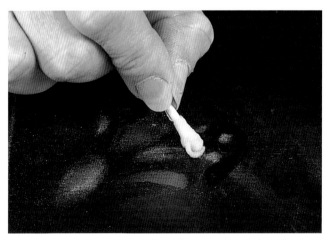

7 To remove excess gilding from around the edges of your design, dip a cotton swab in mineral spirits and use it to clean up the powder. When you're finished, brush a coat of oil-based varnish over the entire piece. After the varnish dries, reinstall the door on the cabinet.

# Child's Playful Table

DESIGNER: KATHERINE AIMONE

*Whether they're drawing or gabbing with a friend over milk and cookies, kids will love hanging out at this table, with its colorful stenciled letters and numbers.*

Small table and chairs

Latex primer

Sandpaper and tack cloth

2- and 3-inch (5 and 7.6 cm) paintbrushes

Latex paints in three colors of your choice (we used bright yellow, green, and blue)

Set of round sponges with handles

Plastic bowls

Number and letter stencils of your choice (available at craft stores)

Paper towels

Cotton swabs

Latex paint or artist's acrylic paint in a couple of accent colors that complement the three main colors (we used dark green and black)

Stick-on alphabet of your choice (available at craft stores)

Oversized tacks (available at craft or office supply stores)

Small hammer

Small artist's paintbrush

## PREPARATION

Prime the table and chairs, and let them dry. Sand lightly and wipe down with a tack cloth before applying a second coat of primer.

1 Paint the table and chairs with the three latex colors, alternating the colors as you wish to make the pieces lively and fun. Follow the lines of the

furniture to guide you. Allow the paint to dry. To stencil numbers and letters on top of the table, pour a bit of each of the three paints and the accent colors into a separate plastic bowl. Dip a round sponge with one of the colors. Dab off the excess paint onto a paper towel.

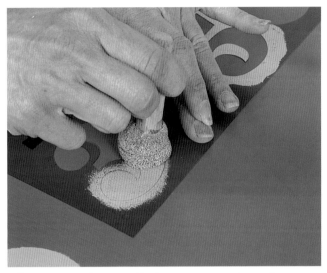

2 Position the stencil where you want it, and pounce a light coat of paint evenly inside the cutout lines. Pounce on as many coats as needed to get the coverage you want.

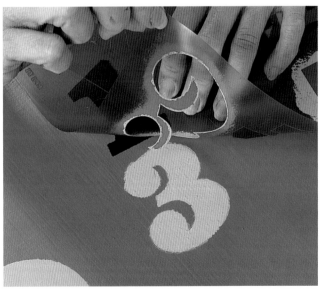

3 Carefully lift the stencil off to reveal the number or letter.

4 If you're unhappy with the edges, you can clean them up with a damp cotton swab or paper towel.

6 Position the stick-on letters of the alphabet on the bottom brace of the table or along an edge of the table.

5 Repeat the stenciling process until you've covered the top of the table with a variety of letters and numbers in different colors and positions. Use the two colors of paint that you used on the other parts of your table and chairs, as well as accent colors to give the design some variety (we used dark green and black).

7 Add decorative tacks on the bottom brace of the table. Make certain that they are hammered in well so they can't be pulled out by a child. Use a small artist's paintbrush to touch up any areas on the table that need it.

# Old-Fashioned High Chair

DESIGNERS: KATHERINE AIMONE AND LYNA FARKAS

*Re-create the charm of an old high chair from grandmother's attic. A crackle finish is easy to do, and replicas of old seed packets on the tray will make vegetables look appealing!*

## YOU WILL NEED

High chair with recessed eating tray

Latex primer

Sandpaper and tack cloth

2- and 3-inch (5 and 7.6 cm) paintbrushes

Light yellow satin latex paint

Replicas of old seed packets

Decoupage glue or artist's acrylic medium

Crackling glaze (comes in two bottles due to two-step process, available at home supply stores)

Handheld electric hair dryer (optional)

Clean, lint-free rag

Oil-based chestnut stain or diluted latex paint of stain consistency

Epoxy resin and catalyst (available at home supply stores)

Sturdy plastic bowl

Latex varnish

Brush latex primer over the high chair and let it dry.
Sand it and wipe it down with the tack cloth before
applying another coat. Brush on two coats of
soft yellow paint and let it dry.

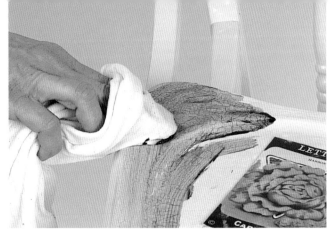

3 Use a clean rag to rub chestnut stain or diluted latex paint over a section of the chair, wiping it off as you go to create an aged look.

1 Place the seed packets on the tray and position them in an appealing way. Remove them, and brush decoupage glue or acrylic medium on the recessed area of the tray. Position them again on top of the tray, and press them into place. Brush a coat of the glue or medium on top of them, and let it dry. Brush on the first coat of crackling glaze over the entire chair, and when tacky, brush on the second coat.

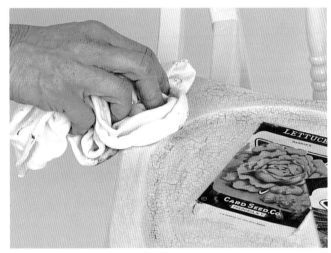

4 Wipe away the stain to reveal the crackle. Continue this process to stain the whole chair. Let it dry overnight.

2 Allow the crackle to dry and cure. If you wish to speed up the drying process, you can use an electric hair dryer.

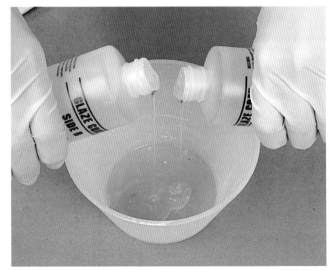

5 Mix equal amounts of epoxy resin with catalyst in a sturdy plastic bowl, and stir for five minutes.

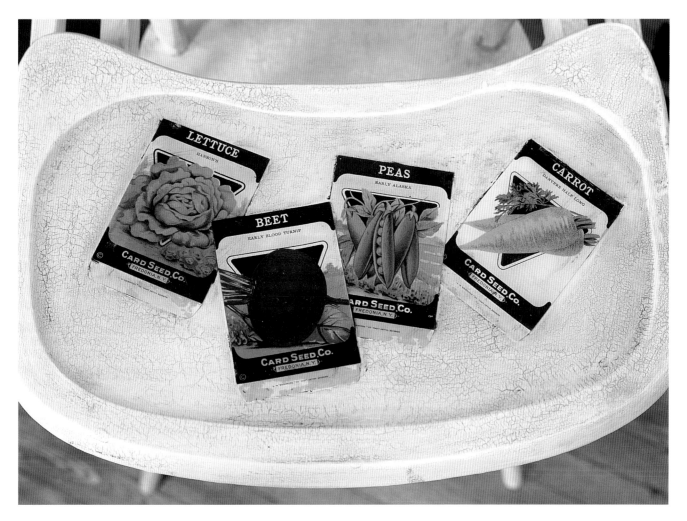

6 With the high chair placed on a level floor, slowly pour the mixture into the recessed area on the tray.

7 Allow the mixture to move and level out on its own. Add as much as you need to cover the interior of the tray with a thick, glossy, easy-to-clean coating. Allow it to dry overnight. After it dries, brush varnish on the other areas of the chair to protect it.

# Delft Tile Sofa Table

DESIGNER: LYNA FARKAS

*Inspired by the look of aged Dutch tiles, this table shows off another faux look with paint.*
*Your friends will have to touch it to believe that the tiles aren't real!*

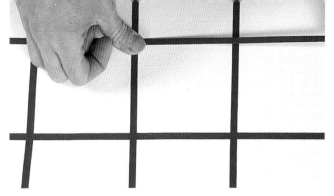

Sofa table with decorative molding on legs

Latex primer

2-inch (5 cm) paintbrushes and small roller with paint tray

Sandpaper and tack cloth

White flat latex paint

Off-white flat latex paint

Ultramarine blue flat latex paint

Small artist's paintbrush

Long metal ruler

Watercolor pencil

¼-inch (6 mm) colored tape (vinyl tape from an auto supply store or narrow masking tape from a craft supply store)

Painter's masking tape (available at home supply stores)

Crackling glaze

Clean, lint-free rag

Template (see page 77)

Carbon paper or graphite transfer paper

Latex varnish

**PREPARATION**

Prepare the table by priming it, sanding it lightly, and wiping it down with a tack cloth before applying a second coat of primer. Paint the table legs with two coats of white paint. Paint the top and sides with two coats of off-white paint.

1  Paint the leg moldings with two coats of ultramarine blue. Clean up the adjoining edges between the blue and white with the small artist's brush. (Allow each first coat of paint to dry before applying the second.)

2  Measure the width and length of the top of your table to figure out the spacing for your tiles, and draw them out with a ruler and watercolor pencil. Keep in mind that all the tiles don't have to be exactly the same size. (For instance, to make the configuration work on our table, we ended up drawing 3 x 3½-inch [7.6 x 8.9 cm] tiles around the border and 3½ x 3½-inch [8.9 x 8.9 cm] tiles in the center.) Apply ¼-inch (6 mm) colored tape over the pencil marks.

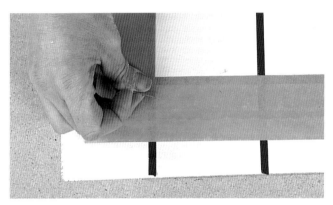

3  Position painter's tape along the edge of the outer tiles to protect them, since you'll paint them a darker color later.

4  Brush a coat of crackle on the middle tiles, and let it dry until it is tacky. Then brush on a coat of white paint. (Try to get a good coat on with one or two strokes so you don't disturb the crackle.) The crackle effect should happen instantly. Allow the crackled

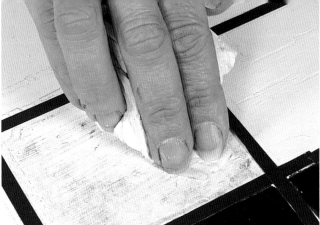

6 Immediately wipe it off to give it a soft, mottled appearance that looks like ceramic glaze.

7 Use the template provided to transfer the rounded motifs onto the tiles with carbon paper or graphite transfer paper and a pen or pencil. Paint the motifs with ultramarine blue paint, and lighten a bit of the paint with white. Then use a small artist's brush to add lighter-valued accents to the motifs.

paint to dry, and then remove the wide painter's tape. Place tape along the same edge, but on the opposite side, to protect the middle tiles. Brush crackle on the outer tiles, and let it dry until tacky. Brush on low-sheen ultramarine blue paint, covering the crackle with one or two thick coats. After it cracks, remove the tape. Allow the paint to dry.

5 Use a cloth to lightly wipe dark blue paint on every other white tile.

8 Use a bit of the off-white paint on a small brush to touch up the edges of the grout to suit your tastes. After it dries, varnish the whole piece to protect it.

# Wardrobe with Dimensional Stenciling

DESIGNER: LYNA FARKAS

*Antique meets contemporary in this tall wardrobe decorated with a unique textured surface.*

## YOU WILL NEED

Wardrobe with doors

Water-based spray varnish

Latex primer

2- and 3-inch (5 and 7.6 cm) paint-brushes and small roller with paint tray

Sandpaper and tack cloth

Templates (see page 77)

Poster board or other heavy paper

Carbon paper or graphite transfer paper

Cutting board

Craft knife

Long metal ruler

Pencil

Low-tack masking tape

Trowel

Texturing paint or joint compound

Sanding block

Clean sea sponge

3-inch (7.6 cm) paintbrush

Latex paints in off-white and taupe

Remove the wardrobe doors. Spray varnish on the interior of the piece and on the back side of the doors. Prime the outside of the piece, including the fronts of the doors. Then lightly sand and wipe down with the tack cloth before applying a second coat of primer.

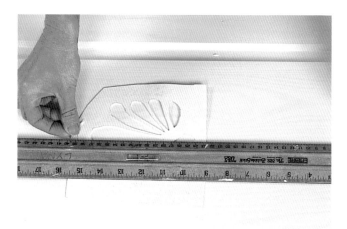

1 Transfer the templates to poster board or other heavy paper with carbon paper. Place each motif on a cutting board, and cut out the designs with the craft knife to create two reverse stencils. Spray the edges of the stencils with varnish to strengthen them. Use the metal ruler and pencil to measure and mark the center of one of the bottom door panels. Position the larger stencil in the center as shown on the finished piece.

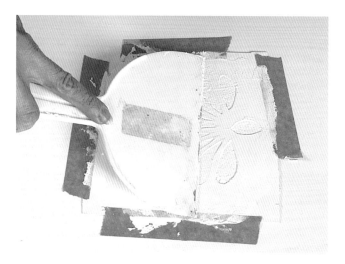

2 Tape the stencil in place, and use the trowel to apply a thin layer of texturing paint over it. Gently work the texture into the cutout sections of the stencil. While the texture is still wet, gently remove the stencil

by lifting one corner and pulling it toward the opposite one. Follow the same steps to create the smaller dimensional motifs on the top door panels.

3 Dab a sea sponge into the texturing paint and discharge the excess onto a paper towel.

4 Lightly pounce the texture in random areas over the entire wardrobe. Allow it to dry overnight.

6 Rinse out your sponge, wring it out until damp, and spread the glaze to soften it. Try to keep a wet edge between sections to avoid dark adjoining lines as you glaze the outside of the wardrobe.

7 Touch up parts on the stenciled areas with a bit of dark paint. After you've glazed and sponged the whole piece, allow it to dry. Spray a coat of varnish over the whole piece to protect the surface.

5 Lightly knock off sharp peaks of texture from the motif with a light sanding. Brush two coats of off-white paint on top of the paint and textured areas, and let them dry. Mix two parts of off-white paint to one part of taupe to make a glaze. Use a brush to apply the glaze to a small section of the piece. Repeat this process in an adjacent area.

# Period Rocker

DESIGNER: LYNA FARKAS

*Buy a new rocker and transform it into a piece that looks like a treasured antique. It's sanded in all the right places to appear as if it's been lovingly used over the years.*

Spindle-back rocker

Sandpaper and tack cloth

Two 2-inch (5 cm) paintbrushes

Oil-based maple stain

Clean, lint-free rags

Flat green latex paint

$\frac{1}{4}$- and $\frac{1}{2}$-inch (6 mm and 1.3 cm) artist's brushes

Dark red and yellow artist's paints in tubes or bottles

Oil-based mahogany stain

## PREPARATION

Sand the rocker and wipe it down with a tack cloth.
With a 2-inch (5 cm) brush, apply maple stain to the whole
chair. With a lint-free rag, wipe off the excess stain.
Allow the chair to dry overnight.

2 Sand the surfaces lightly in areas to expose the stain and make the chair appear as if it has worn naturally over time.

1 Use a 2-inch (5 cm) brush to apply a light coat of green paint to the whole chair. Allow the paint to dry.

3 Using the illustration as a guide, use the smaller brushes to begin painting decorative motifs on the headrest.

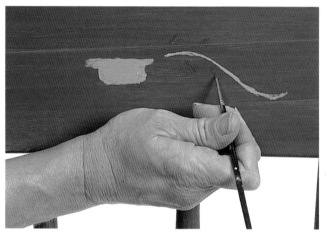

4 Painting freehand lines will lend a rustic look to your piece. Don't worry about making perfect lines.

6 After they dry, lightly sand the painted areas to give them an aged appearance.

7 Paint a light coat of mahogany stain over a section of the chair.

5 Paint the rungs, the legs, and the seat with decorative motifs as well.

8 Wipe off the excess with a clean rag. Continue this process until you've applied stain to the entire chair.

# Copper-Finish Chest

DESIGNER: DERICK TICKLE

*The subtle metallic effect of corroded copper leaf makes this chest of drawers a posh addition to any room. You'll be surprised at how easy it is to do!*

## YOU WILL NEED

Tall chest of drawers

Sandpaper and tack cloth

Latex primer

2- and 3-inch (5 and 7.6 cm) paintbrushes

Light yellow latex paint

Wood conditioner

Soft paintbrush for applying stain

Moss-green water-based stain

Clean, lint-free rags

Water-based size (available in craft supply stores)

Foam brush

Copper leaf sheets (available in craft supply stores)

Cotton gloves

Soft cosmetic brush

Clean cotton rags

White vinegar

Clear plastic film (found in grocery stores)

Paper towels

Water-based varnish

Decorative brass drawer knobs

Lightly sand all surfaces of the chest, and wipe it down with the tack cloth. Remove the drawers and take off the existing knobs. Prime the fronts of the drawers, and allow them to dry before applying two coats of light yellow paint. Use a brush to apply wood conditioner to the rest of the piece

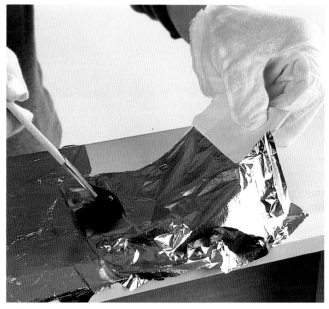

3 Lightly smooth out the wrinkles with the soft brush. Overlap leaf sheets to cover the rest of the drawer and the remaining drawer fronts. Allow the leaf to dry a couple of hours, then use a soft brush to lightly rub off excess leaf.

1 Use the soft brush to apply colored wood stain to the sides and top of the chest, then wipe it down with a lint-free cloth to even out the color. The stain allows the natural wood grain to show through.

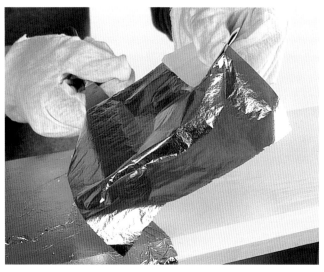

4 Stand the drawers on their ends, and allow the copper leaf to harden overnight. Soak several cotton rags in vinegar, and wring them out until they are damp. Crumple the rags and place them loosely over the copper leaf. Cover them with clear plastic film to keep them from drying out.

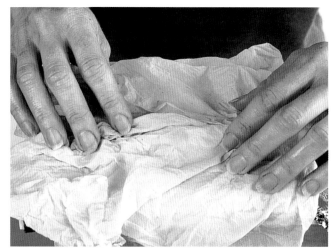

2 Use a foam brush to apply the water-based gold size to the drawer fronts on top of the yellow paint. Let it dry for 30 minutes. Put on the cotton gloves. Insert a sheet of copper leaf between a folded piece of paper, and position it along the edge of one of the drawers.

5 After about two hours, remove a corner of one of the rags to reveal the patina. If the pattern is to your liking, remove the rags; or, if you want a more pronounced patina, leave them a while longer. Once you've taken the rags off, remove any excess vinegar with paper towels, and let the patina dry. Apply two coats of water-based varnish to the drawers and the whole piece. Attach the decorative brass knobs to the drawers, and reassemble the chest.

# Collage of Color Shelves

DESIGNER: LYNA FARKAS

*Use sponges to apply overlapping shapes and colors that are then blended beneath a stain wash.*

## YOU WILL NEED

Shelf unit with removable shelves

Sandpaper and tack cloth

3-inch (7.6 cm) paintbrush

Pickling stain (available at home supply stores)

Clean, lint-free rag

Wide masking tape

Latex house paints in several colors of your choice (we used blue, red, yellow, and purple)

Shallow, wide containers for holding paints (such as disposable plates)

Sponges in various sizes and shapes (available at home supply stores)

Paper towels

Remove the shelves from the unit, and sand all surfaces before wiping them down with the tack cloth. Brush pickling stain on all surfaces, and wipe off the excess with a clean rag as you go. The stain will be absorbed by the wood and lighten when it is dry.

3 Begin in one of the corners of the back of the shelf, and press the sponge firmly and evenly to release the paint.

1 Place masking tape around the edges of the back of the shelf to prevent paint from getting on the top and sides of the inside. Put a dab of each paint color in each shallow container. Add a small amount of water to thin the paint.

4 Use the end of your brush to stipple the paint into the corners that the sponge won't cover. Sponge more of the same shape and color in the quadrant where you're working, leaving space around the shapes.

2 Dip one of the sponges in one of the paint colors and discharge the excess paint onto a paper towel, or add a smooth coat of paint to the sponge with a paintbrush before discharging it.

5 Add more shapes and colors with various sponges.

6 Overlap the colors as you work, allowing the colors to blend together. Don't worry about making perfect prints. Keep in mind that you're making a "collage" of color. After you've covered the back of the shelf with your design, allow it to dry completely. Brush on a coat of pickling stain to soften the colors, and wipe off the excess stain.

7 Apply another coat until you have the effect you want. Allow the stain to dry completely before placing the shelves back in the unit.

# Vinegar-Painted Jelly Cabinet

DESIGNER: MICHELLE MICHAEL

*Vinegar painting emerged in the 19th century as an inexpensive way for artisans to emulate the look of fancy graining on furniture and woodwork. This piece shows off bright colors using this old technique.*

## YOU WILL NEED

Cabinet with door

Latex primer

2- and 3-inch (5 and 7.6 cm) paint-brushes and small roller with paint tray

Sandpaper and tack cloth

Cream-colored satin latex paint

Clear spray varnish

Measuring spoons

Blue, purple, and green powdered pigments (available at art supply stores)

Liquid dish detergent

Plastic bowls

Vinegar

Sugar

Oil-based varnish

Low-tack masking tape

Large feather (such as a turkey feather)

Remove the door from the cabinet and the knob from the door. Sand and prime the outside of the cabinet, the door, and the knob. Sand lightly and wipe with the tack cloth before applying a second coat of primer. Brush on two coats of cream-colored paint over the primed areas. Apply a coat of spray varnish to the inside of the cabinet and the back of the door.

1 Assemble your materials for vinegar painting: measuring spoons, powdered pigments, dish detergent, vinegar, plastic bowls, sugar, and brushes.

2 Mix 1 cup (.24 L) of vinegar with a drop of dish detergent. To mix your first color for vinegar painting, measure out 1 tablespoon (14 g) of powdered pigment into a shallow bowl. Then mix in ¼ teaspoon (1 g) of sugar. Add 1 teaspoon (5 mL) of the vinegar/detergent mix to the pigment and blend it to a paint-like consistency. If it seems too thick, add more vinegar in ¼-teaspoon (1.25 mL) increments until you achieve the desired consistency, keeping in mind that if it is too thin, the paint will run.

3 Place the door on a flat surface, and brush an even coat of the vinegar paint within the confines of the molding or another area of your choice. (Vinegar evaporates quickly, so you'll need to mix in more vinegar as you work.)

4 Hold a brush perpendicular to the painted surface, and swirl the paint to make a pattern, as shown. Apply this color and pattern to any other sections of the piece as you wish (such as the top and sides). Allow the paint to dry. (If you are not happy with your design, you can remove it with water because vinegar paint is water soluble.) Then brush on a coat of oil-based varnish over the color. Allow the varnish to dry. (It is important that you do this before you move on, to prevent the vinegar painting from smearing as you work on other sections.)

5 As needed, place low-tack tape over the areas that you've already painted with color to protect them while you add the next color to sections of the piece. Mix up the next color using the same formula that you did for the first (see step 2). Brush an even coat of the next color onto an area of your choice. Use a brush to create a scalloped pattern by working the brush back and forth as you move down the surface. Paint other areas with this color and recreate the pattern.

6 After the varnish dries, you're ready to add your final color to various sections. Tape off any edges as needed to protect the painting you've already done. Mix up the third color, and brush it on a section of your choice. Use the feather to stipple or pounce the paint to create a pattern, moving it around as you work. The result will be an uneven, varied pattern. Add this final color to the remaining blank areas, and after it dries, complete it with a coat of varnish. In narrow areas (such as the top of our cabinet), you can use the vinegar paint as you would a stain, brushing it on until you achieve a look that you like. After you've painted the final sections, apply a coat of varnish on top, and let it dry. Then apply one more coat of varnish to the whole piece.

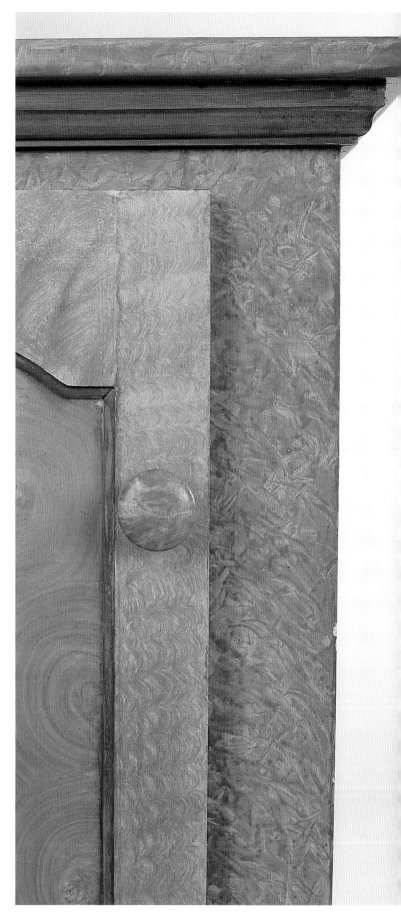

# Leafy Adirondack Chair

DESIGNER: LYNA FARKAS

*A summer afternoon will be even better when you're reclining in this lovely chair that looks*
*as though it has soft shadows cast by tree branches. The technique is so simple*
*and fun that you'll want to paint a pair of them!*

## YOU WILL NEED

Adirondack-style chair

Sandpaper and tack cloth

Plastic drop cloth

Piece of poster board or mat board

Artificial ferns (available at craft stores)

Light green, medium green, and blue-green spray enamel paints

Paint mask

Wide masking tape

Spray varnish

## PREPARATION

Place your chair in a well-ventilated space or outside. Sand the chair and wipe it down with the tack cloth. Place it on a plastic drop cloth.

2 Protect your lungs by wearing a paint mask. Spray the chair all over with the lighter paint, using a wide, sweeping motion. Then, go back and cover all the edges and crevices of the chair, both front and back. Let the paint dry. Hold leaves against the back and seat of the chair, keeping an area blank at the top to lend the effect of sunlight on the chair. Spray paint over sections of the leaves to make an airbrush effect.

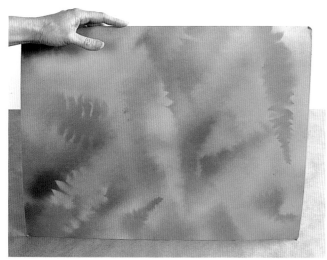

1 Do a test of your spray on a piece of poster board or mat board to get a feel for using the leaves as a reverse stencil. Spray on a coat of lighter paint first as your base coat, and then follow up by masking off areas with leaves and spraying on top of them until you get an effect that you like.

3 Lift off the leaf to reveal the reverse stencil.

5 Use another color to add more complexity to the design.

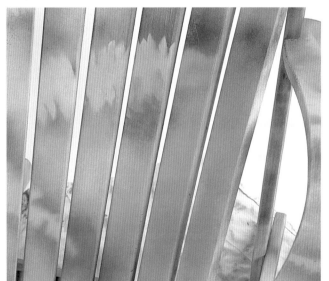

4 Add areas of color without the leaves to create a layered effect.

6 Spray the arms of the chair using the same technique. When you're satisfied with your design, spray on a protective coat of varnish.

# Faux Brick Garden Chest

DESIGNER: LYNA FARKAS

*This eye-catching and unusual chest emulates the look of a broken plaster wall
with brick beneath it. It might look tricky to do, but it isn't.*

## YOU WILL NEED

Chest with lid that opens

Latex primer

2- and 3-inch (5.1 and 7.6 cm) paintbrushes

Sandpaper and tack cloth

Light-gray flat latex paint

Long ruler

Pencil

1-inch (2.5 cm) masking tape

Trowel

Texturing paint or joint compound

Clean sea sponge

Paper towels

Tubes or bottles of artist's paint in red, brown, dark umber, white, and dark green

Craft knife

Off-white satin latex paint

Dark red satin latex paint

Low-sheen varnish

## PREPARATION

Paint the outside of the chest (top, sides, back, and front) with primer, and allow it to dry. Lightly sand and wipe off the piece with the tack cloth before applying a second coat of primer. Brush two coats of light gray paint on the front of the chest, and let it dry.

1 Use the long ruler to draw pencil lines indicating a broken-away pattern of bricks on half of the front of the chest (our bricks are $3\frac{1}{2}$ x $7\frac{1}{2}$ inches [8.9 x 19 cm]). You don't need to cover the whole chest with a brick pattern, because only part of it will be exposed (see finished photo). Cover the lines with masking tape, and extend the tape up and over the top of the chest. Lightly trowel on a thin layer of texturing paint or joint compound into the taped sections, and stipple it with a wide paintbrush as you work to create a brick-like texture. Overlap the edges around the bricks with more texture paint or joint compound to create the effect of plaster broken away from a wall. Continue to add texture around the rest of the chest in this same way, covering the gray paint and side of the chest. To create a varied texture on the non-bricked areas, stipple the surface with a damp sea sponge before lightly skimming the trowel over the peaks to flatten them slightly. Allow all the textured areas to dry overnight.

2 Drybrush a light coat of red paint from a tube or bottle on the bricks.

3 Dab a damp sea sponge with a mixture of brown and red paint and discharge the excess on a paper towel. Randomly dab more color on the bricks.

4 Lightly brush on more brown and some dark umber paint. Follow up by dabbing the color again with the sponge. Continue this process of layering and blending until you're satisfied with the outcome.

5 Carefully remove the tape, using the craft knife to cut away the taped areas if they are covered with

texture. Add a bit of water to the dark umber paint to make a wash. Dip the smaller paintbrush in the wash and wipe the excess off on a paper towel. Dry brush the grout areas between the bricks.

6 Use the same dry-brush technique to add white to the area between the bricks. Finish off the effect with a bit of randomly added dry-brushed green that lends the effect of mold.

7 Paint all the areas of texture on the chest, except for the bricks, with a coat of off-white paint. Allow the paint to dry. Mix up more of the dark umber wash, and brush it on top of the non-bricked texture in one section.

8 Use the sponge (or a rag) to gently wipe off some of the wash and soften the look of the paint to create the illusion of age. Continue doing this in sections.

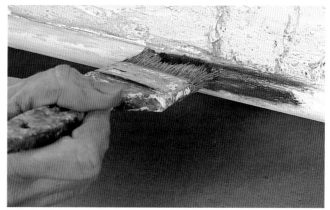

9 Paint the top of the chest and the bottom molding with two coats of the dark red latex paint. After the paint dries completely, paint a coat of low-sheen varnish over the entire chest to protect it.

# Faux Marquetry Bench

DESIGNER: LYNA FARKAS

*The technique known as "stain marquetry" allows the beauty of the natural wood grain to shine through a semi-transparent layer of painted and rubbed stains.*

Spindle-backed bench

Sandpaper and tack cloth

Wood conditioner

2- and 3-inch (5 and 7.6 cm) paintbrushes

Oil-based stains in oak, antique maple, chestnut, and mahogany

Several clean, lint-free rags

Enlarged template or hand-drawn design of your own for the seat of the bench

Carbon paper

Pen, pencil, or other pointed tool for tracing

Craft knife

Several small artist's brushes

Oil-based stains in yellow and green

Oil-based varnish

**PREPARATION**

Sand the bench and wipe it down with the tack cloth. Brush a coat of wood conditioner over the entire piece, and wait about 20 minutes before you begin staining.

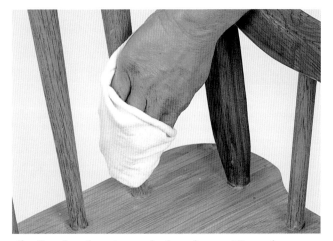

1 Brush oak stain on the bench seat. Use a clean rag to wipe off the excess stain. Let it dry. Use another clean rag to wipe antique maple stain on the spindles at each end and the middle spindles, as well as the hand rest and leg support spindles. Rub chestnut stain on the remaining back spindles and the side spindles of the bench. Rub mahogany stain on the frame, arms, and legs of the bench. Let it dry.

2 Position the template or hand-drawn design on the seat of the bench. Place carbon paper underneath it, and trace it with a pen or pencil or other pointed tool. Remove the template.

3 With a craft knife, slightly score (cut) the leaves and berries to keep the stains that you'll apply from bleeding into each other.

4 Use small artist's brushes to paint the design with the four wood stains as well as the yellow and green stains.

5 Paint around the edges of the design with a second coat of oak stain, and apply a second coat to the rest of the seat to darken it.

# High Table and Chairs with Mosaic

DESIGNER: KATHERINE AIMONE

*The bright, bold colors of this matching table and chairs were inspired by an African-American quilt.*
*The random nature of the sponged mosaic lends a jazzy touch.*

## YOU WILL NEED

Round high table and chairs
(our chairs have woven seats)

Latex primer

2- and 3-inch (5 and 7.6 cm)
paintbrushes

Sandpaper and tack cloth

Two latex paints in highly contrasting
shades (we used black and bright
apple green)

Old toothbrush or other small,
stiff brush (optional)

Several latex or acrylic paints as accent
colors (only small amounts are needed)

Paper towels or clean rag

Set of round sponges with handles

Long metal ruler

Pencil

## PREPARATION

Prime the table and chairs, and allow
them to dry. Sand them lightly and wipe
them down with a tack cloth before
applying another coat of primer.

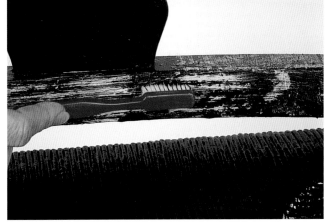

1 Decide which areas of the chairs you wish to paint with each of the contrasting main colors, following the natural lines of the pieces. If you wish, select one area (such as the back of the chair) to paint with a light/dark combination of colors before distressing the area. To do this, paint the area with a coat of the lighter color, and allow it to dry. Paint the darker color on top, allow it to dry slightly, and then use the small, stiff brush to randomly scratch off the darker coat to reveal the lighter coat beneath it.

3 Use accent colors to wipe over lighter areas of the piece and create an antique look. Don't be afraid to experiment and layer the colors until you get an effect that you like; you can always wipe the paint off with a damp paper towel if you want to change it.

2 Paint the rest of the chair with the lighter color. Paint the table with black or another color of your choice, leaving certain areas unpainted, such as decorative features around the edge, molding on the pedestal, or the feet. Use the second contrasting color (green or other) to paint the accent areas. Use a heavily loaded brush to paint the seats of the chairs with several coats of paint, pouncing the brush up and down to coat and cover the woven strands.

4 On the top of the table, use your contrasting and accent colors along with the round sponges to create a mosaic-like pattern. You can begin this pattern by finding the center of the table and drawing a rough underlying structure for your mosaic with a pencil and ruler (for instance, we began with a simple cross in the middle). To create the mosaic, load round sponges with paint and press them onto the tabletop, turning them slightly to release the paint onto the surface. Mix and layer colors as you wish. Don't be afraid to experiment!

5 After the main areas of your design dry, you can add a bit of paint to the surface with the sponge to create a blurred effect. Here, we put a small amount of black paint on the sponge, pressed it onto an existing circle, and then turned it clockwise to create a subtle, overlaid spiraling design on top.

6 To add more dimension to the design, randomly pounce a light coat of contrasting paint on top of various areas of the mosaic design.

# Jazzed-Up Writing Table

DESIGNER: DERICK TICKLE

*Taking his cue from a spirited piece of wallpaper, this designer added painted piano keys to this table. A smashing way to liven up any room!*

Writing table

Sandpaper and tack cloth

Sanding sealer or clear shellac

Long ruler

2- and 3-inch (5.1 and 7.6 cm) paintbrushes

Wallpaper primer

Clean, lint-free rags

Wood stains in two colors and black that coordinate with your wallpaper

Low-tack masking tape

Small sponge roller

White and black latex paint

Painter's masking tape

Fine-tipped black marker

$\frac{1}{2}$-inch (1.3 cm) black vinyl tape

Craft or utility knife

Wallpaper with musical motif

Wallpaper paste

Pasting brush

Smoother or sponge

Non-yellowing satin varnish

## PREPARATION

Lightly sand the table to remove any rough edges or splinters, then use a tack cloth to remove the dust. Mark off a 2-inch (10.2 cm) border around the sides and back edge of the tabletop. To ensure even color and prevent blotchiness when you stain the table, apply one coat of sanding sealer or clear shellac to all parts of the table except the panel inside the border, where you'll apply wallpaper. Let it dry for two hours. Apply one coat of wallpaper primer to the panel on the tabletop, and let it dry. Use a fine sandpaper to sand all the surfaces you sealed, making sure to sand only in the direction of the natural wood grain.

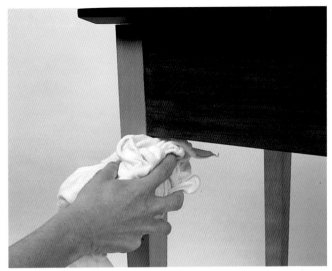

1 Use clean cloths to apply colored wood stains (including the legs, drawer, knob, and the marked border in black) to all areas of the table but the top central panel. When the stains dry, apply a second coat, if necessary. The stain should allow the natural wood grain to show through.

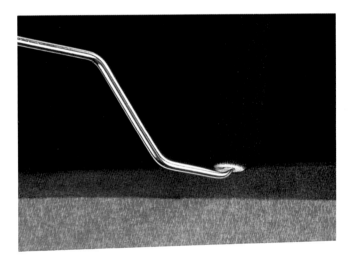

2 Mark a line 4 inches (10.2 cm) in from the front edge of the tabletop between the two black side borders. Inside the 4-inch (10.2 cm) border and along the line that you drew, position a line of masking tape. Use a small roller to paint a narrow strip of black along the line (most of this will be covered by the wallpaper later). Allow the paint to dry.

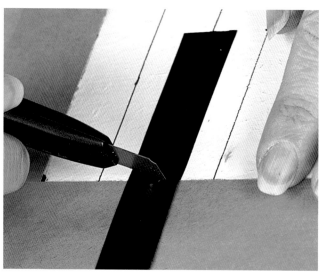

3 Mask off the line on the reverse side and paint the 4-inch (10.2 cm) border and the edge of the front of the table with white paint. Allow the paint to dry and remove the tape.

5 Use ½-inch (1.3 cm) black tape to form the keys, following the sequence shown in the finished photo. Tape each black key in place and cut off the excess with a sharp craft knife.

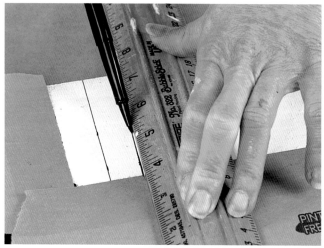

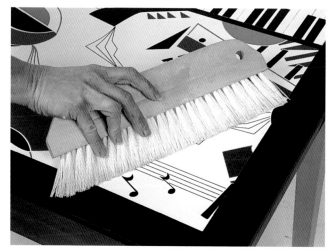

4 Use wide painter's tape to mask off the keyboard area. Draw lines with a fine-tipped black marker that are ¾ inch (1.9 cm) apart and continue the lines down the white edge on the table's front.

6 Cut a piece of wallpaper 2 inches (5.1 cm) wider and longer than the central panel. Paste the paper and apply it, smoothing out any air pockets with a smoother or damp sponge. With the metal ruler and craft or utility knife, carefully trim the panel to size. Make sure that the edges are firmly pressed down and no air bubbles remain. Remove any excess paste from the surrounding areas, and let everything dry overnight. Finish the whole piece with two coats of varnish to provide a durable and washable surface.

# Exotic Patterned Bed

DESIGNER: MICHELLE MICHAEL

*Another twist on vinegar painting uses simple finger painting to achieve
a rich and intriguing pattern.*

1 Mask off the areas that you plan to decorate with vinegar painting. Brush two coats of cream-colored paint on the sections and let them dry.

## YOU WILL NEED

Bed frame with headboard and baseboard

Latex primer

Sandpaper and tack cloth

2- and 3-inch (5 and 7.6 cm) paintbrushes and paint roller with tray

Painter's masking tape

Cream-colored satin latex paint

Liquid dish detergent

Vinegar

Measuring cup

Shallow container for mixing vinegar paint

Measuring spoons

Black dry pigment (available at art supply stores)

Sugar

Talcum powder

Oil-based varnish

Clean, lint-free rag

Black satin latex paint

2 To make vinegar paint, mix a cup (.24 L) of vinegar with a drop of dish detergent. In a separate, shallow dish, mix 1 tablespoon (14 g) of black pigment powder with $1/4$ teaspoon (1 g) sugar. Add a teaspoon (5 mL) of the vinegar mix to the pigment and blend it to a paint consistency. If you feel it is too thick, add more vinegar $1/4$ teaspoon (1.25 mL) at a time until you achieve the desired consistency. If it's too thin, the paint will run when applied to the vertical surface.

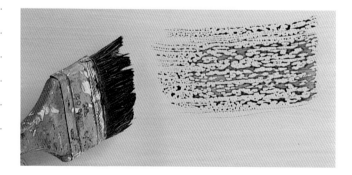

3 Apply the black vinegar paint to a small section of the bed. (You need to work quickly in small sections because the vinegar paint will dry fast.) If it beads up on the surface, as shown in the photo, you can remedy this problem.

## PREPARATION

Prime the whole bed, and let it dry. Lightly sand the surfaces and wipe them off with the tack cloth before applying a second coat of primer.

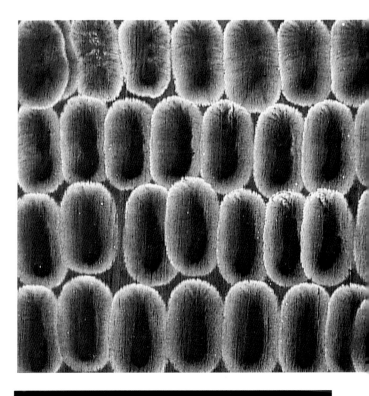

4 If the paint beads, you can use a brush to apply the talcum powder to the paint surface before adding the paint. Another method to prevent it from beading up is applying a coat of oil-based varnish over the paint and letting it dry before using the vinegar paint.

5 Once the vinegar paint application looks consistent, you're ready to begin making the pattern, beginning at the top of the area you've painted.

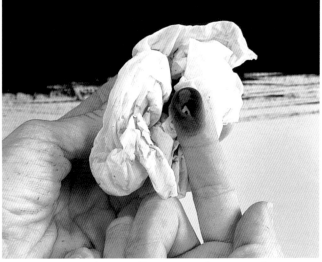

6 To do this, use your thumb or index finger to make a horizontal, even row of prints in the paint. Continue directly below this row so that your prints touch one another without overlapping.

7 Wipe your finger off occasionally to avoid paint buildup. Continue until the section is done. Brush more vinegar paint on the adjoining section and repeat the process. (Vinegar evaporates quickly, so you'll need to mix more vinegar in the pigment as you work.) If you aren't happy with your design, you can remove it with water and a lint-free rag, since vinegar paint is soluble in water. Once the paint is completely dry, usually in about three to four hours, varnish the patterned areas with oil-based varnish, and allow it to dry completely. Paint the remaining areas of the bed with two coats of the cream-colored paint or the black satin paint. (We painted the panels cream and the rails and top of the bed black.)

# Faux Finish Screen

DESIGNER: LYNA FARKAS

*This stately screen shows off four faux finishes within the boundaries of a stenciled rope design. You'll need some help from a carpenter to make the panels, or you can do them yourself by following the instructions. Use the template on page 78 as a guide for cutting the panels.*

2 sheets of $^3/_4$-inch (1.9 cm) x 4 x 8-foot (1.2 x 2.4 m) smooth plywood

Sawhorses with large piece of plywood on top or other large work surface

Jigsaw

C-clamps

Sandpaper and tack cloth

Small handheld sander (optional)

Latex primer

Paint tray and several paint rollers as well as smaller sponge rollers

1-inch-wide (2.5 cm) flat paintbrush

Semi-gloss latex paint in dark blue-green, medium yellow, and antique gold

Long ruler

Pencil

Low-tack masking tape

Spoon

Water-based clear glaze medium

Plastic containers

Clean, lint-free rags (available at home supply stores)

4-inch-wide (10.2 cm) paintbrush

3-inch-wide (7.6 cm) paintbrush

Wallpaper brush

Fine-toothed rubber hair comb

Rope template (see page 78)

Clear acetate or heavy paper

Carbon paper or graphite transfer paper

Fine-tipped black marker

Craft knife

Cutting mat

Stencil adhesive spray

Cosmetic sponges

Tubes of artist's acrylic paint in gold and antique gold

Acrylic varnish

6 double-acting/butterfly hinges with screws, each hinge measuring $^3/_4$ x 1$^3/_4$ inches (1.9 x 4.4 cm)

Electric drill/screwdriver

Clamp one of the pieces of plywood into place on top of your work surface, and use a jigsaw to cut out two 18-inch-wide (45.7 cm) wood panels following the illustration on page 78 for the top cuts. Repeat with the other large piece of plywood to make two more panels. Make the panels a height of your choice—ours measures 5½ feet (1.7 m) at the highest point. Lightly sand the edges, fronts, and backs of each panel, and wipe them down with the tack cloth. Use a roller to apply an even coat of primer to both sides of each panel. Apply primer to the sides of the panels with the 1-inch-wide (2.5 cm) paintbrush. When all areas have dried, lightly sand the panels again. Use a clean roller to apply two coats of dark blue-green paint to the back of each panel, allowing the paint to dry between coats. Use another roller to paint the fronts and sides with two coats of medium yellow paint. Allow the paint to dry.

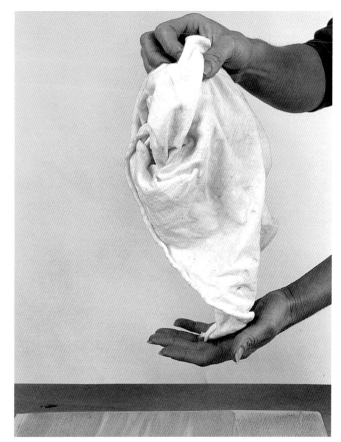

1 Line up the panels on your work surface, floor, or against a wall. Beginning on the first panel, use the long ruler to mark a diagonal line from the upper left corner to the bottom right corner. Repeat on the fourth panel. On the second and third panels, mark the diagonals from the top right corner to the bottom left corner. Run a strip of masking tape underneath each of the lines. Burnish the tape with a spoon so that paint won't seep under it. Mix one part blue-green paint

with three parts glaze in a plastic container. To create a green "rag roll" finish on the top sections and sides of panels one and two, apply the blue-green wash with a paint roller. Next, hold up a damp, lint-free rag, and drop it into your hand so that it bunches up.

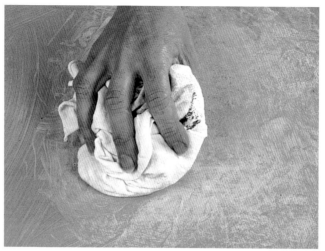

2 Place the rag on the edge of the panel, and roll it in different directions until you've covered all of the blue-green area. Try not to roll over areas twice. Allow the panels to dry while you move on to the other two panels.

4 Use loose strokes and the 4-inch-wide (10.2 cm) paintbrush to paint the gold wash on the top sections of the third and fourth panels, moving from the top of each panel down to the tape. Paint the adjoining sides as well. Dab the painted surfaces with a bunched up damp rag to soften the appearance of the paint strokes. Allow all four panels to dry completely.

3 Make a gold wash by stirring one part antique gold paint with three parts glaze medium in one of the plastic containers.

5 Remove the tape from each of the panels. Tape ABOVE the lines this time, protecting the areas that you've just painted. Use the same gold wash you used in step 3 to paint even, vertical strokes with the 3-inch-wide (7.6 cm) paintbrush on the bottom sections and sides of panels one and two. Starting at the top of each newly painted section, hold the wallpaper brush parallel to the screen, and drag it all the way down the panel. Wipe the brush with a rag before making the next adjacent sweep down the panel. Continue until both sections are done.

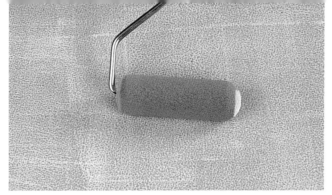

top edge of the diagonal line on the first panel. Dip the end of a cosmetic sponge into a small amount of gold acrylic paint. Press the sponge onto a paper towel to wipe off any excess paint, then dab and stipple the sponge on the open areas of the template. Carefully lift off the stencil, and allow the paint to dry.

6 Sponge roll the same blue-green wash on the bottom sections and sides of panels three and four.

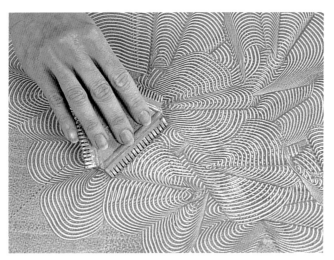

7 Place the teeth of the rubber comb on the surface of the panel, and carve scallops in the glaze until the sections are covered with the pattern. Keep wiping the comb to keep the scallops consistent. Allow the glaze to dry. Remove the tape.

9 Reposition the stencil on top of the areas you've already painted so that you fill in the blank areas of the rope. Sponge with the antique gold acrylic paint to make a continuous line. Continue to reposition and sponge until you've completed the diagonal. Clean the stencil in the sink with hot water and a sponge. Allow the paint to dry. Stencil the rope designs on the remaining three panels, following the diagonal lines. When completely dry, use a sponge roller to apply a coat of acrylic varnish to the top and sides of the screen. Allow it to dry thoroughly. Hinge the screen together as shown in the finished photo.

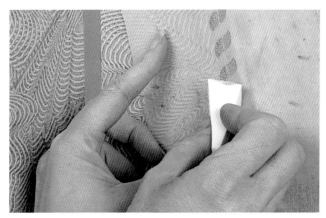

8 Use carbon paper or graphite transfer paper to transfer the rope template to heavy paper, or use a black marker to trace it onto acetate. Place the template on the cutting mat, and use the craft knife to cut out the shapes with a craft knife. Spray the back of the stencil with stencil adhesive spray, and center it on the

# Templates

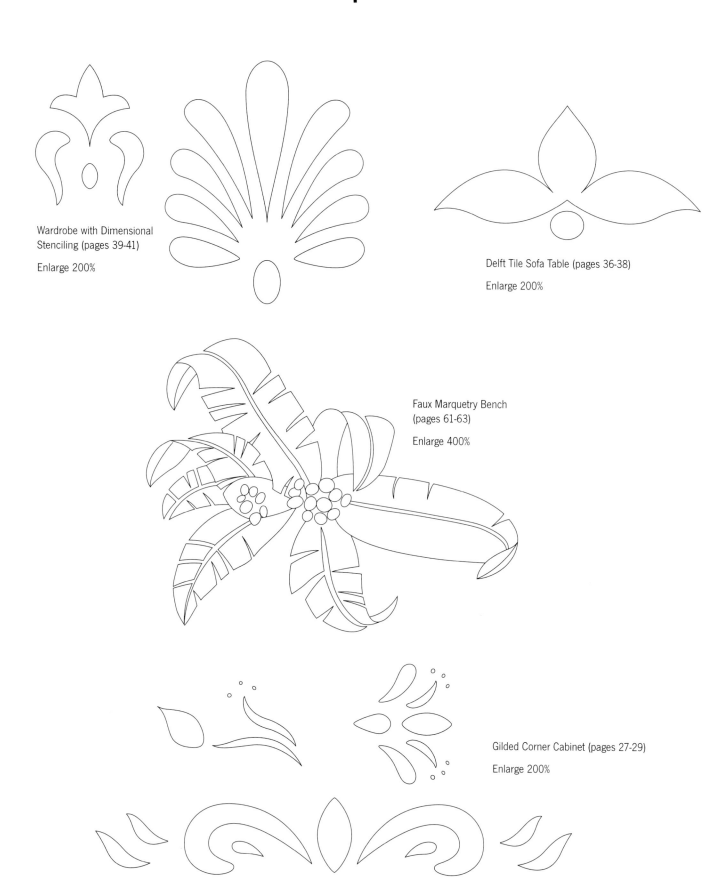

Wardrobe with Dimensional
Stenciling (pages 39-41)

Enlarge 200%

Delft Tile Sofa Table (pages 36-38)

Enlarge 200%

Faux Marquetry Bench
(pages 61-63)

Enlarge 400%

Gilded Corner Cabinet (pages 27-29)

Enlarge 200%

Period Rocker (pages 42-44)

Enlarge 200%

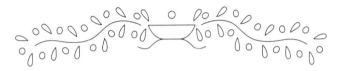

Period Rocker (pages 42-44)

Enlarge 400%

Faux Finish Screen, Rope template
(pages 73-76)

Enlarge 200%

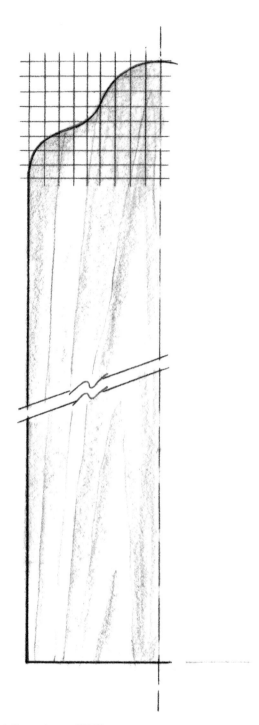

Faux Finish Screen (pages 73-76)

Guide for screen panels, each square equals 1 inch (2.5 cm).
Adjust height as you wish.

## Acknowledgments

To my editor, Katherine Aimone, thanks for your inspiration and for pulling this book together so smoothly, even with a time crunch.

To Stacey Budge, the art director for the book, for your input and help during the shoots and a wonderful layout.

To Steve Mann, the photographer for the book, thanks for your attention to detail.

To my dear friends and colleagues, Derick Tickle and Michelle Michaels, for taking my furniture design ideas and running with them, creating wonderful pieces to share with us.

A special thanks to Marshall Manche, owner of Wood You Furniture in Asheville, North Carolina, for providing designer support.

Thanks to Sepp Leaf in New York for supplying gilding materials and information.

Thanks to Rob Pulleyn, Terry Taylor, and Chris Bryant of Lark Books for allowing us to use their terrific homes for photography.

## Designers

Derick Tickle teaches decorative painting and restoration in Asheville, North Carolina. Trained in England as an apprentice, he is an examiner and advisor in decorative painting for the City and Guilds of London. He has run workshops and seminars for TV set designers, interior decorators, and professionals in Britain, New Zealand, and the United States.

Michelle Michael's background is in interior design and historic preservation. In addition to decorative painting and restoration work, she is a historic preservation consultant. Michelle enjoys combining painting techniques and traditions of the past with today's colors to create fun pieces of decorative art.

Katherine Aimone is an editor for Lark Books who enjoys doing creative work in collage and painting on the side.

## Biography

Lyna Farkas is a graduate of City and Guilds of London's program of Decorative Art and Restoration and is now the accessor for their North American school. Through her business, In the Spirit of Decorum, in Asheville, North Carolina, Lyna creates personalized interiors for homes, showrooms, and commercial sites as well as accent pieces such as floor cloths and furniture. She also teaches, writes, and consults in her field. Her work has been featured in the showrooms of Bernhardt Furniture as well as Martha Stewart. With Paige Gilchrist, she coauthored the book titled *Creative Wallpapering* (Lark Books, 2003).

# Index